PRAYER

OF ▪ THE

SICK

LTP

LITURGY
TRAINING
PUBLICATIONS

ACKNOWLEDGMENTS

The English translation of the psalms and the Canticle of Mary, Canticle of Simeon, and Canticle of Zechariah from the *Liturgical Psalter* © 1994, International Committee on English in the Liturgy, Inc. All rights reserved.

Scripture passages from the New Revised Standard Version Bible, copyright © 1989, Division of Christian Education of the National Council of the Churches of Christ in the United States of America.

Collect prayer for the Litany of the Blessed Virgin Mary, "We turn to you for protection," "Strengthen me," "Mother of Sorrows" and Memorare from *Catholic Household Blessings and Prayers,* copyright © 1988, United States Catholic Conference, Washington, D.C.

"Litany of Christ the Healer" from *Pray Like This: Materials for the Practice of Dynamic Group Prayer,* compiled by William G. Storey, copyright © 1973, Claretian Publications, Inc., Chicago, Ill.

"A Litany of Modern Ills" from *The Covenant of Peace,* compiled by John P. Brown and Richard York. Copyright © 1971, Morehouse-Barlow Co., Wilton, Conn.

"For Doctors, Nurses" and "For Nursing Home Residents" are original texts by David Philippart. All rights reserved.

"Lord Jesus Christ, by your patience" and "O God, the source of all health" from the *Book of Common Prayer.*

"Stabat Mater," translated by Anthony G. Petti, copyright 1971, Faber Music Ltd., London, England.

Every effort has been made to determine the ownership of all texts and to make proper arrangements for their use. We will gladly correct in future editions any oversight or error that is brought to our attention.

This book was compiled by David Philippart. Deborah Bogaert was the production editor. It was designed and hand-lettered by Kerry Perlmutter and typeset in Trajan and Galliard by Karen Mitchell. Janice Kiska did the artwork. *Prayers of the Sick* was printed in the United States of America.

PRAYERS OF THE SICK © 1995 Archdiocese of Chicago: Liturgy Training Publications, 1800 North Hermitage Avenue, Chicago IL 60622-1101; 1-800-933-1800; orders@ltp.org; fax 1-800-933-7094; All rights reserved. Website www.ltp.org.

Library of Congress Catalog Card Number: 95-80260

ISBN 1-56854-130-9

SICK

PSALM 23

The Lord is my shepherd,
I need nothing more.
You give me rest in green meadows,
setting me near calm waters,
where you revive my spirit.

You guide me along sure paths,
you are true to your name.
Though I should walk in death's dark valley,
I fear no evil with you by my side,
your shepherd's staff to comfort me.

You spread a table before me
as my foes look on.
You soothe my head with oil;
my cup is more than full.

Goodness and love will tend me
every day of my life.
I will dwell in the house of the Lord
as long as I shall live.

FOREWORD

We get hurt. We wear down. The lungs, the eyes, the memory and all the many limbs and organs that compose us break or ache. Gloomy moods come over us then: pity for ourselves, depression, anger. But hope can come, too, and courage, and sometimes peace.

All of this is heard in the prayers of our tradition. Many psalms are the desperate or bitter pleading of the sick. They call upon God to be near, to heal by sharing in the pain. In the scriptures, Job questions God about suffering, Isaiah sees an end to sickness, and with word and deed, with touch and breath and spit and mud, Jesus heals. In every place and time, we the church anoint the sick with oil and share the one bread even with those who cannot assemble for Mass. Thus we are made one and remain one, a single body of many parts.

The world may at times seem to count the sick as useless — unable to produce, unable to consume anything but medical resources. But to the church — as to God — the sick are precious. Those who suffer carry in their bodies the image of the crucified Christ. We come to know that suffering need not be meaningless and that God hears the prayers of the sick as the words of Christ on the cross. So the vocation — the ministry — of the sick Christian is to pray always.

From our psalms, scriptures and other traditions we have words to shape that prayer. Those gathered in this book have been arranged in categories to help you choose words for particular occasions. But don't be restricted by the suggested uses. Use this book as seems best to you. Add to these words the hymns and prayers that you know by heart and cherish. And let the scriptures here lead you to further reading in the Bible as you are able. Pray with others when this is possible. Ask gently and without coercion if those who live with you or come to visit would like to stop for a moment, recognize God's presence, give thanks and praise, and intercede for those — including yourself—who are in need. ∎

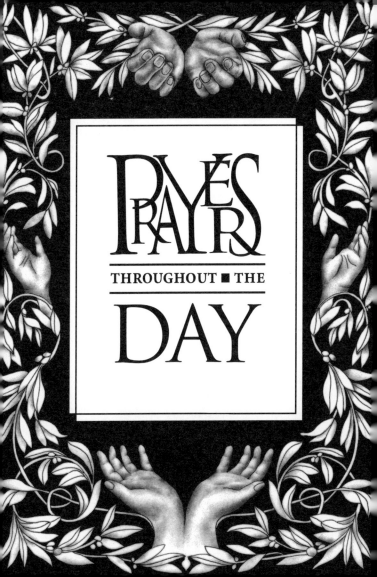

PRAYERS

THROUGHOUT ∎ THE

DAY

MORNING PRAYER

This order of prayer may be said upon waking, or before or after breakfast.

> **O Lord, open my lips,**
> **and my mouth shall declare your praise.**

The Sign of the Cross

You may dip your hand in water to make the sign of the cross.

> **In the name of the Father**
> **and of the Son and of the Holy Spirit.**

You may sing a hymn that you remember and cherish, even sing it alone softly.

Psalm 63

God, my God, you I crave;
my soul thirsts for you,
my body aches for you
like a dry and weary land.
Let me gaze on you in your temple:
a vision of strength and glory.

Your love is better than life,
my speech is full of praise.
I give you a lifetime of worship,
my hands raised in your name.
I feast at a rich table,
my lips sing of your glory.

On my bed I lie awake,
your memory fills the night.
You have been my help,
I rejoice beneath your wings.

Yes, I cling to you,
your right hand holds me fast.

Let those who want me dead
end up deep in the grave!
They will die by the sword,
their bodies food for jackals.
But let the king find joy in God.
All who swear by truth be praised,
every lying mouth be shut.

*Pause for silent prayer. If you feel well enough,
you may read a short passage from the Bible
now. Use your own Bible, or use a scripture passage found elsewhere in this book (on pages
33 and 38, for example).*

The Canticle of Zechariah

Praise the Lord, the God of Israel,
who shepherds the people and sets them free.

God raises from David's house
a child with power to save.
Through the holy prophets
God promised in ages past
to save us from enemy hands,
from the grip of all who hate us.

The Lord favored our ancestors
recalling the sacred covenant,
the pledge to our ancestor Abraham,
to free us from our enemies,
so we might worship without fear
and be bold and just all our days.

And you, child, will be called
Prophet of the Most High,
for you will come to prepare
a pathway for the Lord
by teaching the people salvation
through forgiveness of their sin.

Out of God's deepest mercy
a dawn will come from on high,
light for those shadowed by death,
guide for our feet on the way to peace.

Intercessions

Pray now for peace in the world, for a deeper spiritual life in your parish and in the diocese, for the pope and the bishops, and for people who are suffering in particular disasters.

The Lord's Prayer

You may hold your hands with palms facing upward while praying the Lord's Prayer. ■

EVENING PRAYER

This order of prayer may be said before or after dinner, or when the sun sets.

O God, come to my assistance.
O Lord, make haste to help me.

The Lighting of a Candle

If you are not using oxygen, you may light a candle to welcome the evening while saying:

Jesus Christ is the light of the world,
a light no darkness can overcome.

You may sing a hymn that you remember and cherish, even sing it alone softly.

Psalm 141:1-5, 8

Hurry, Lord! I call and call!
Listen! I plead with you.
Let my prayer rise like incense,
my upraised hands, like an evening sacrifice.

Lord, guard my lips,
watch my every word.
Let me never speak evil
or consider hateful deeds,
let me never join the wicked
to eat their lavish meals.

If the just correct me,
I take their rebuke as kindness,
but the unction of the wicked
will never touch my head.
I pray and pray
against their hateful ways.

Lord my God, I turn to you,
in you I find safety.
Do not strip me of life.

Pause for silent prayer. If you feel well enough,
you may read a short passage from the Bible
now. Use your own Bible, or use a scripture pas-
sage found elsewhere in this book (on pages 61
and 62 for example).

The Canticle of Mary

I acclaim the greatness of the Lord,
I delight in God my savior,
who regarded my humble state.
Truly from this day on
all ages will call me blest.

For God, wonderful in power,
has used that strength for me.
Holy the name of the Lord!
whose mercy embraces the faithful,
one generation to the next.

The mighty arm of God
scatters the proud in their conceit,
pulls tyrants from their thrones,
and raises up the humble.
The Lord fills the starving
and lets the rich go hungry.

God rescues lowly Israel,
recalling the promise of mercy,
the promise made to our ancestors,
to Abraham's heirs for ever.

Intercessions

Pray now for peace in the world, for a deeper spiritual life in your parish and in the diocese, for the pope and the bishops, and for people who are suffering in particular disasters.

The Lord's Prayer

You may hold your hands with palms facing upward while praying the Lord's Prayer. ■

NIGHT PRAYER

This order of prayer may be said before going to sleep.

**May Almighty God give us a restful
night and a peaceful death.**

*You may sing a hymn that you remember and
cherish, even sing it alone softly.*

Psalm 131

Lord, I am not proud,
holding my head too high,
reaching beyond my grasp.

No, I am calm and tranquil
like a weaned child
resting in its mother's arms:
my whole being at rest.

Let Israel rest in the Lord,
now and for ever.

The Canticle of Simeon

Lord, let your servant
now die in peace,
for you kept your promise.

With my own eyes
I see the salvation
you prepared for all peoples:

a light of revelation for the Gentiles
and glory to your people Israel.

Invocation to Mary

The final prayer of the day is customarily to the Blessed Mother.

> Hail, holy Queen, Mother of mercy,
>   hail, our life, our sweetness, and our
>   hope.
> To you we cry, the children of Eve;
> to you we send up our sighs,
> mourning and weeping
>   in this land of exile.
> Turn, then, most gracious advocate,
> your eyes of mercy toward us;
> lead us home at last

and show us the blessed fruit
   of your womb, Jesus:
O clement, O loving, O sweet
Virgin Mary!

The Sign of the Cross

We end the day the way we began it, with the
sign of the cross.

May the almighty and merciful Lord,
   the Father and the Son
   and the Holy Spirit,
bless and keep us. Amen. ■

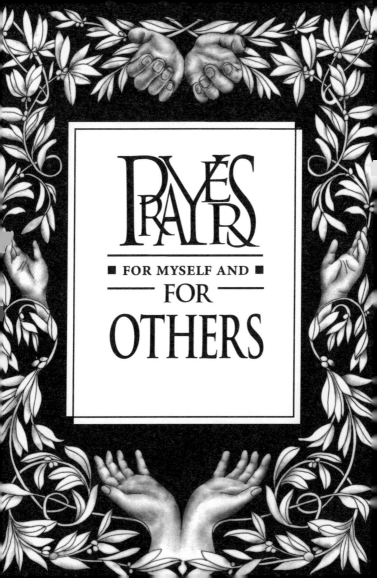

PRAYERS

■ FOR MYSELF AND ■

— FOR —

OTHERS

LITANY OF CHRIST THE HEALER

Lord Jesus, Son of David and Son of God
heal us and save us.

Lord Jesus, who bore our griefs
and carried our sorrow
heal us and save us.

Lord Jesus, who went about preaching
the Good News and curing
all kinds of disease and sickness
heal us and save us.

Lord Jesus, who raised to life
the daughter of Jairus,
and the only son
of the widow of Nain
heal us and save us.

Lord Jesus, who cured Simon Peter's
mother-in-law of a fever
and the woman suffering
from hemorrhages
heal us and save us.

Lord Jesus, who delivered the Gadarene
demoniacs, and the tormented daughter
of the Canaanite woman
heal us and save us.

Lord Jesus, who cured the centurion's
paralyzed servant and the epileptic
boy who could not speak
heal us and save us.

Lord Jesus, who restored the sight
of Bartimaeus, the blind beggar
of Jericho and who purified
many lepers
heal us and save us.

Lord Jesus, who cured the man with the
withered hand, and who made
cripples whole again
heal us and save us.

Lord Jesus, who commanded your disciples
to lay hands on the sick
and anoint them with oil
heal us and save us.

Lord Jesus, who ordered your disciples
to cast out demons in your name
heal us and save us.

*Here mention, one by one, the names of all the
sick whom you wish to pray for, including yourself. Then say:*
heal us and save us. ▪

LITANY OF THE BLESSED VIRGIN MARY

Lord, have mercy.	**Lord, have mercy.**
Christ, have mercy.	**Christ, have mercy.**
Lord, have mercy.	**Lord, have mercy.**
God our Father in heaven	**have mercy on us.**
God the Son, Redeemer of the world	**have mercy on us.**
God the Holy Spirit	**have mercy on us.**
Holy Trinity, one God	**have mercy on us.**
Holy Mary	**pray for us.**
Holy Mother of God	**pray for us.**
Holy Virgin of virgins	**pray for us.**
Mother of Christ	**pray for us.**
Mother of the church	**pray for us.**
Mother of divine grace	**pray for us.**
Mother most pure	**pray for us.**
Mother of chaste love	**pray for us.**
Mother most amiable	**pray for us.**
Mother most admirable	**pray for us.**

Mother of good counsel	**pray for us.**
Mother of our Savior	**pray for us.**
Virgin most wise	**pray for us.**
Virgin most powerful	**pray for us.**
Virgin most merciful	**pray for us.**
Virgin most faithful	**pray for us.**
Mirror of justice	**pray for us.**
Seat of wisdom	**pray for us.**
Cause of our joy	**pray for us.**
Shrine of the Holy Spirit	**pray for us.**
Glory of Israel	**pray for us.**
Vessel of honor	**pray for us.**
Mystical rose	**pray for us.**
Tower of David	**pray for us.**
House of gold	**pray for us.**
Ark of the covenant	**pray for us.**
Gate of heaven	**pray for us.**
Morning star	**pray for us.**
Health of the sick	**pray for us.**
Refuge of sinners	**pray for us.**
Comfort of the afflicted	**pray for us.**
Help of Christians	**pray for us.**

Queen of angels	**pray for us.**
Queen of patriarchs and prophets	**pray for us.**
Queen of apostles and martyrs	**pray for us.**
Queen of confessors and virgins	**pray for us.**
Queen of all saints	**pray for us.**
Queen conceived without sin	**pray for us.**
Queen assumed into heaven	**pray for us.**
Queen of the rosary	**pray for us.**
Queen of peace	**pray for us.**

Lamb of God, you take away
the sins of the world **have mercy on us.**

Lamb of God, you take away
the sins of the world **have mercy on us.**

Lamb of God, you take away
the sins of the world **have mercy on us.**

Pray for us, holy Mother of God.
That we may become worthy
   of the promises of Christ.

Let us pray.

> Eternal God,
> let your people enjoy constant health
>   in mind and body.
> Through the intercession of the Virgin
>   Mary
> free us from the sorrows of this life
> and lead us to happiness in the life to
>   come.
> Grant this through Christ our Lord.
> **Amen.** ∎

FOR THE WORLD: A LITANY OF MODERN ILLS

From hunger and unemployment, and from
   forced eviction:
   Good Lord, deliver us.
From unjust sentences and unjust wars:
   Good Lord, deliver us.
From neglect by parents, neglect by children,
   and neglect by callous institutions:
   Good Lord, deliver us.
From cancer and stroke, ulcers,
   madness and senility:
   Good Lord, deliver us.
From famine and epidemic, from pollution of
   the soil, the air and the waters:
   Good Lord, deliver us.
From segregation and prejudice, from
   harassment, discrimination and brutality:
   Good Lord, deliver us.

From the concentration of power in the hands of
  ignorant, threatened or hasty leaders:
    Good Lord, deliver us.
From propaganda, fads, frivolity and
  untruthfulness:
    Good Lord, deliver us.
From arrogance, narrowness and meanness,
  from stupidity and pretence:
    Good Lord, deliver us.
From boredom, apathy, and fatigue, from lack
  of conviction, from fear,
  self-satisfaction and timidity:
    Good Lord, deliver us.
From the consequences of our own folly:
    Good Lord, deliver us.
From resignation and despair,
  from cynicism and manipulation:
    Good Lord, deliver us.
Through all unmerited suffering, our own and
  that of others:
    Good Lord, deliver us.

Through the unending cry of all peoples for
   justice and freedom:
   Good Lord, deliver us.
Through all concern and wonder,
   love and creativity:
   Good Lord, deliver us.
In our strength and in our weakness, in
   occasional success and eventual failure:
   Good Lord, deliver us.
Alone and in community, in the days of action
   and the time of our dying:
   Good Lord, deliver us.
Deliver us, Good Lord, by opening our eyes and
   unstopping our ears, that we may hear your
   word and do your will:
   Good Lord, deliver us. Amen. ■

FOR DOCTORS, NURSES AND OTHER HEALTHCARE WORKERS

Lord Jesus Christ,
you cured the bodies, nursed the souls and
  healed the hearts of all the sick
  who came to you in faith.
Strengthen all doctors, nurses and healthcare
  workers (especially N. and N.).
Give them wisdom and skill, patience and
  determination, compassion and sympathy
that they may work to cure, speak to soothe, and
  touch to heal in the power of the Holy Spirit.
Amen. ■

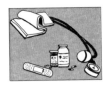

FOR NURSING HOME RESIDENTS

Lord Jesus Christ,
hope of the elderly and the infirm,
the aged prophets Simeon and Anna
longed for your birth and were not disappointed.
Carried to the Temple in your mother's arms,
you brought them consolation and redemption.
Come this day to comfort and redeem
all who live in nursing homes
(especially N. and N.).
Do not delay, Lord! Do not disappoint us!
Then shall all the aged praise you
    with blessed Anna,
and sing with Simeon his song of joy:
"Now, Master, you have kept your word;
    I go in peace
having seen your salvation." ▪

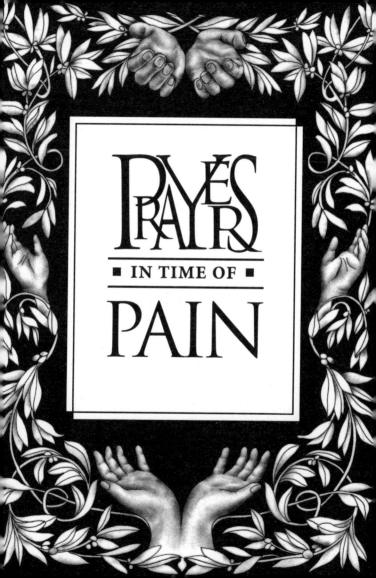

PRAYERS

■ IN TIME OF ■

PAIN

Pity me, Lord,
I hurt all over;
my eyes are swollen,
my heart and body ache.

Grief consumes my life,
sighs fill up my days;
guilt saps my strength,
my bones dissolve.
  —*Psalm 31:10 – 11*

Lord Jesus Christ, by your patience in suffering you hallowed earthly pain and gave us the example of obedience to your Father's will: Be near me in my time of weakness and pain; sustain me by your grace, that my strength and courage may not fail; heal me according to your will; and help me always to believe that what happens to me here is of little account if you hold me in eternal life, my Lord and my God. Amen.

I consider that the sufferings of this present time are not worth comparing with the glory about to be revealed to us. For the creation waits with eager longing for the revealing of the children of God; for the creation was subjected to futility, not of its own will but by the will of the one who subjected it, in hope that the creation itself will be set free from its bondage to decay and will obtain the freedom of the glory of the children of God. We know that the whole creation has been groaning in labor pains until now; and not only the creation, but we ourselves, who have the first fruits of the Spirit, groan inwardly while we wait for adoption, the redemption of our bodies.

— *Romans 8:18 – 27*

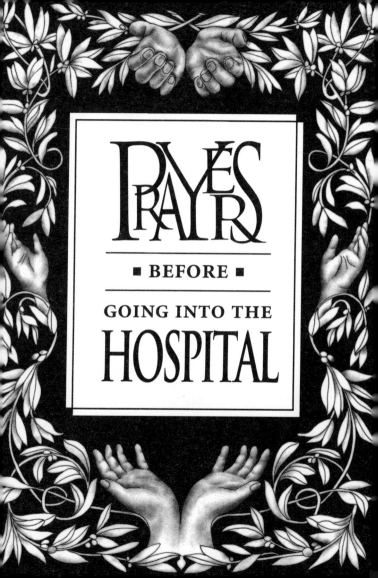

PRAYERS

■ BEFORE ■

GOING INTO THE

HOSPITAL

Care for me, God, take care of me,
I have nowhere else to hide.
Shadow me with your wings
until all danger passes.

— *Psalm 57:2*

If I look to the mountains,
will they come to my aid?
My help is the Lord,
who made earth and the heavens.

May God, ever wakeful,
keep you from stumbling;
the guardian of Israel
neither rests nor sleeps.

God shields you,
a protector by your side.
The sun shall not harm you by day
nor the moon at night.

God shelters you from evil,
securing your life.
God watches over you near and far,
now and always.

— *Psalm 121*

We turn to you for protection,
holy Mother of God.
Listen to our prayers
and help us in our needs.
Save us from every danger,
glorious and blessed Virgin. ■

So we do not lose heart. Even though our outer nature is wasting away, our inner nature is being renewed day by day. For this slight momentary affliction is preparing us for an eternal weight of glory beyond all measure, because we look not at what can be seen but at what cannot be seen; for what can be seen is temporary, but what cannot be seen is eternal.

—*2 Corinthians 4:16–18*

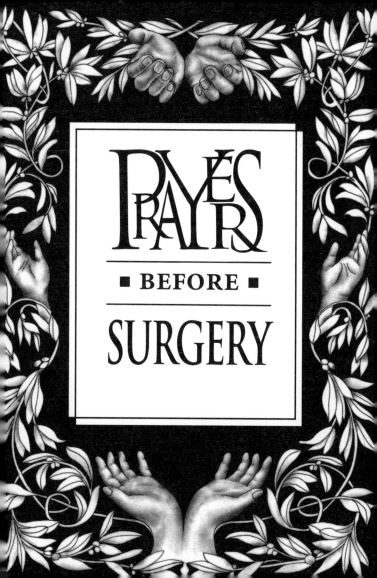

PRAYERS

■ BEFORE ■

SURGERY

*The prayer of someone who is faint and pours
out complaints to the Lord.*

Hear my prayer, Lord,
let my cry reach you.
Do not turn from me
in my hour of need.
When I call, listen,
answer me at once.

For my days dissolve like smoke,
my bones are burned to ash.
My heart withers away like grass.
I even forget to eat,
so consumed am I with grief.
My skin hangs on my bones.

Like a gull lost in the desert,
like an owl haunting the ruins,
I keep a solitary watch,
a lone bird on a roof.
All day my enemies mock me,
they make my name a curse.

For bread, I eat ashes,
tears salt my drink.
You lifted me up in anger
and threw me to the ground.
My days pass into evening,
I wither like the grass.

But you, Lord, preside forever,
every age remembers you.
Rise with mercy for Zion,
for now is the time for pity.

God has broken me in my prime,
has cut short my days.
I say: "My God, do not take me.
My life is only half-spent,
while you live from age to age."

Long ago you made the earth,
the heavens, too, are your work.
Should they decay, you remain.
Should they wear out like a robe,
like clothing changed and thrown away,

you are still the same.
Your years will never end.

May your servants' line last forever,
our children grow strong before you.
— *Psalm 102:1 – 14, 24 – 29*

Remember, most loving Virgin Mary,
never was it heard
that anyone who turned to you for help
was left unaided.

Inspired by this confidence,
though burdened by my sins,
I run to your protection
for you are my mother.
Mother of the Word of God,
do not despise my words of pleading
but be merciful and hear my prayer.
Amen. ■

For those suffering desperate or lost causes:

Saint Jude Thaddeus, apostle and martyr, pray
for me!

For those suffering from any form of cancer:

Saint Peregrine Laziosi, patron of those suffering
from cancer, pray for me!

For women suffering breast cancer:

Holy martyr Agatha, who lost your breasts to
the torturer's knife, pray for me!

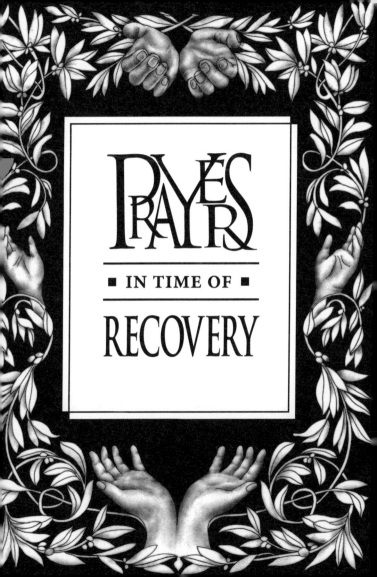

PRAYERS

■ IN TIME OF ■

RECOVERY

Glory be to the Father
and to the Son
and to the Holy Spirit,
as it was in the beginning,
is now,
and ever shall be,
world without end. Amen.

I am filled with love,
for the Lord hears me;
the Lord bends to my voice
whenever I call.

Death had me in its grip,
the grave's trap was set,
grief held me fast.
I cried out for God:
"Please, Lord, rescue me!"

Kind and faithful is the Lord,
gentle is our God.
The Lord shelters the poor,
raises me from the dust.
Rest once more, my heart,
for you know the Lord's love.

God rescues me from death,
wiping my tears,
steadying my feet.
I walk with the Lord
in this land of the living.

I believe, even as I say,
"I am afflicted."
I believe, even though I scream,
"Everyone lies."

What gift can ever repay
God's gift to me?
I raise the cup of freedom
as I call on God's name!
I fulfill my vows to you, Lord,
standing before your assembly.

Lord, you hate to see
your faithful ones die.
I beg you, Lord, hear me:
it is I, the servant you love,
I, the child of your servant.
You freed me from death's grip.

I bring a gift of thanks,
as I call on your name.
I fulfill my vows to you, Lord,
standing before your assembly,
in the courts of your house,
within the heart of Jerusalem.

Hallelujah! ∎

   —Psalm 116

PRAYERS

— ABOUT —

▪ TERMINAL ▪
ILLNESS

Your suffering is Christ's suffering. Pray this psalm, from which Jesus took his last words while dying on the cross.

God, my God,
why have you abandoned me —
far from my cry, my words of pain?
I call by day, you do not answer;
I call by night, but find no rest.

I am poured out like water,
my bones are pulled apart,
my heart is wax melting within me,
my throat baked and dry,
my tongue stuck to my jaws.
You bring me down to the dust of death.

There are dogs all around me,
a pack of villains corners me.
They tear at my hands and feet,
I can count all my bones.
They stare at me and gloat.
They take what I wore,
they roll dice for my clothes.

Lord, do not stay far off,
you, my strength, be quick to help.
Save my neck from the sword,
save my life from the dog's teeth,
save me from the lion's jaws,
save me from the bull's horns.

You hear me.
  —*Psalm 22:1 – 3, 15 – 22*

Seek God's face and long for the beatific vision.

One thing I ask of the Lord,
one thing I seek:
to live in the house of God
every day of my life,
caught up in God's beauty,
at prayer in his temple.

The Lord will hide me there,
hide my life from attack:
a sheltering tent above me,
a firm rock below.

O God, listen to me;
be gracious, answer me.
Deep within me a voice says,
"Look for the face of God!"

So I look for your face,
I beg you not to hide.
Do not shut me out in anger,
help me instead.

Do not abandon or desert me,
my savior, my God.
If my parents rejected me,
still God would take me in.

I know I will see
how good God is
while I am still alive.
Trust in the Lord. Be strong.
Be brave. Trust in the Lord.
   —*Psalm 27:4–5, 7–10, 13–14*

*Sing this song, the Stabat Mater, to join your
pain to that of Jesus and Mary and to enlist
their aid.*

At the cross her station keeping,
Mary stood in sorrow, weeping
When her Son was crucified.

While she waited in her anguish,
seeing Christ in torment languish,
bitter sorrow pierced her heart.

Christ she saw with life-blood failing,
All her anguish unavailing,
Saw him breathe his very last.

Virgin, in your love befriend me,
At the Judgement Day defend me.
Help me by your constant prayer.

Savior, when my life shall leave me,
Through your mother's prayers receive me
With the fruits of victory.

Let me to your love be taken,
Let my soul in death awaken
To the joys of Paradise. ■

[Job said:] "Do not human beings have a hard service on earth, and are not their days like the days of a laborer? Like a slave who longs for the shadow, and like laborers who look for their wages, so I am allotted months of emptiness, and nights of misery are apportioned to me. When I lie down I say, 'When shall I rise?' But the night is long, and I am full of tossing until dawn. My flesh is clothed with worms and dirt; my skin hardens, then breaks out again. My days are swifter than a weaver's shuttle, and come to their end without hope. Therefore I will not restrain my mouth; I will speak in the anguish of my spirit; I will complain in the bitterness of my soul."

—*Job 7:1–6, 11*

[Job said]: "For I know that my Redeemer lives, and at the last will stand upon the earth; and after my skin has been thus destroyed, then in my flesh I shall see God, whom I shall see on my side, and my eyes shall behold, and not another. My heart faints within me!"

—*Job 19:25–27*

One of the criminals who were hanged there kept deriding Jesus and saying, "Are you not the Messiah? Save yourself and us!" But the other rebuked him, saying, "Do you not fear God, since you are under the same sentence of condemnation?" Then he said, "Jesus, remember me when you come into your kingdom." [Jesus] replied, "Truly I tell you, today you will be with me in paradise."

—*Luke 23:39–40, 42–43*